this strand of pearls
belongs to:

Lauren

date: September 10, 2001

Love... Mom

♡ THANK you for being my <u>lovely</u>, inside and out, precious daughter. Please do me a huge favor and live an enchanted life. No one deserves it more than you, dolly. <u>No</u> one!

Love,
Mom...

Forever and always your most loyal fan and cheerleader.

xox

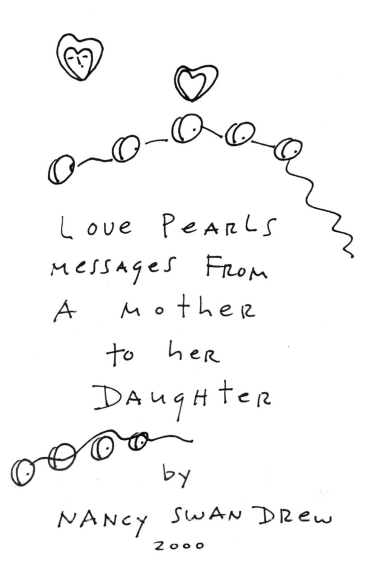

Love Pearls
messages From
A Mother
to her
Daughter

by

NANCY SWAN DRew
2000

Ten Speed Press
Celestial Arts
Berkeley/ Toronto

Celestial Arts
P.O. Box 7123
Berkeley, CA. 94707
Library of Congress Cataloging
in Publication Data on file
with the publisher.

0-89087-983-4
A Heart + Star Book
First printing, 2000
Printed in Hong Kong
1 2 3 4 5 6 7 · 04 03 02 01 00

Dedication

To my daughters
♡ Anna Ryan Drew
And
♡ Maggie Adare Drew
May you never
be without your
Mother's pearls...
they belong to you.
"A"
is for Always
xox

Live Noble Dreams,
Now
And
Always, darlin!

NAME _ _ _ _ _ _ _ _ _ _ _

Noble dreams

xox

HONOR

who you are and who
you will become.
Leave room in your
busy life for those
who Ad_ore you...
just in case you ever
question your magic!

Study the past, search for what you still do not know, HUG the present, and Hail the Future with a Heart-penned map of Hope. Give yourself permission to re-route your sojourn as weather permits.

Hope

NAME - - - - - - - - - - -

N
W ← → E
S

Live and
EAt Richly... wisely!

Enjoy Green Vegetables,
washed Fruit!

Include Herbs in
your life... they Are magic!

Take quiet walks,
smell the earth.

Plant seeds, tend
to them.

Choose Real over
Fake (No Additives!)
Read Labels.

Remove plastic covers
from Lampshades,
use your good
china,
wear
fine or faux
jewels to the
grocery... And

Remember to tell all
those you Love how
much you do treasure
them, each and every
day.

xox

Believe in the goodness of recycling... share your "stuff" with Goodwill... Save spare change for a night at the bowling alley or a day at the beach. Enjoy fads for what they are... All rockin rollin gals should wear bell bottoms at least once!

Buy and wear
Good
Shoes.
A L W A Y S !

WHOAH!

FASHION is
not worth
injury!!

Practice knowing the grand CANYON DiFFeRence between Happiness and PLeasure!

One will Last and the other will travel Far from your daily Rodeo.

Remember to wear a hat and gloves in cold weather. Boots, too! In hot weather, embrace the shade and do not join a nudist colony, unless of course you REALLY want to... because AFTER ALL, it is your life, darlin, NOT MINE!

*

MAKE lists of

things to do, perhaps

in the order of their

importance, and then

have the enormous

FUN

of crossing them off...

so that you may

begin a brand new

List of Productivity!!

grocery
bills
letters
mom
the cinema

Read teeny tiny Fine print as BOLd PRiNT. Look At contents, expiration dates, warnings, side effects, And promises. keep your spectAcles HANdy And crystAl clear!

NEVER... *.

EVER

be hesitant to
ASK FOR HELP
when you need it!
Your beautiful spirit
is cloaked in AN
ARMY of love and
goodwill... ever Ready,
At your beck and call.

S.O.S.

Friends   Family

♡
X
O
X

MANNERS... *

TRy not to chew with your mouth Wide open. (mercy)

TRy not to eat with your elbows owning the table.

TRy not to eat so FAst that conversation is impossible.

And, dARliN, for HEAVEN's sAke, enjoy A NAPkiN oR two.

xox

The two words
"PARDON Me"
ARE A brilliANt
courtesy,
even when undeserved.
Be ever so generous
with your
"PARDON Me's"!

this matters!

dArliN...

When you meet A
brand New FAce...
extend your hand
(A firm shake is not
solely for politiciANs
And CEOs) And Look
the person squarely
in the eyes. Make
sure that when
you ask them how
they Are... you mean
·it·.

* PRActice
(iN the MiRRUR iF
NECeSSARY)   *

SmiLinq

to All those souRed
lemoNs you do Not
pARticulARly FAvoR.

Stop
the clock long
e n o u g h
to take a spot of
T E A . . .

in excellent company
or with your sweet
self.
Take Respite!

Study your intuitive
Self like A scientist...

Beam As your own
lighthouse on Foggy trips...

Let your universe
★ sparkle ★
with
understanding...

And Sweet darlin,
what you can't
understand... cast
off to sea.

bah.bye

? ? ? ? ?

Find
Creatively
Personal
ways to manage
those passions that
SpitFire
toward temper fits
of Rage!

...JOG, Jump Rope,
go to the movies,
Sing out loud to
ELVIS AND TINA
TURNER while driving
N the parking lot
At WAL-MART.

✶

Sweet daughter
of mine...

✶ Bend like a willow
And After All the
Storms...

Standing you shall
Be...

A wiser, sturdier

✶ TREE.

If your Heart seems
a little bored and stalls
in the town of...
♪ Stucksville...
try changing your
Hair-do, radio station,
or socks before
making any Huge
OVERHAULS!!

Think
darlin,
think!

Be
creative

ALL
RISK
should be studied
with A detective's
PROWESS...
And then, just FOR
LUCK,
double - checked by
those you Love And
trust !!

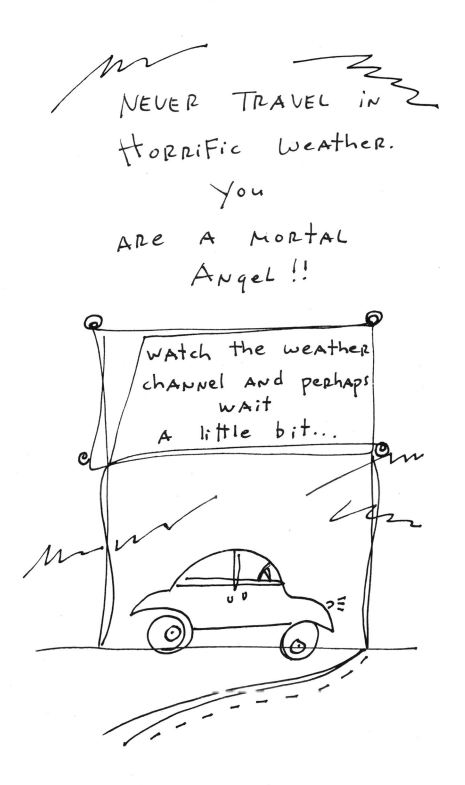

Good
FRiendships
will only be second
Best to the one
And only ORIGINAL
FAmily
who loves you so!
Love both of these
Two cAmps of loyAL
HeArts well. Yes?
(even though one mAy
be A bit FRuitier thAn
the other.)
x o x

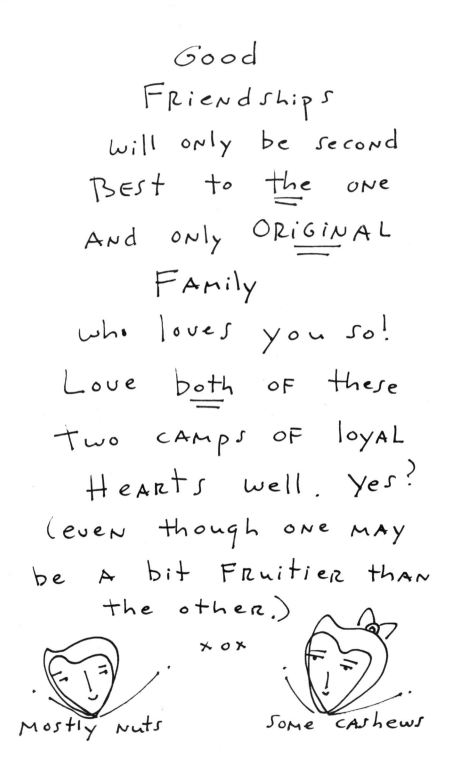

Mostly Nuts   Some cAshews

MAKING FUN with
others can be Hilarious...

MAKING FUN OF
others can wound
the HUMAN Spirit...
Always
know
the diFFeRence.
And leave the company
of Meanness.

Live in the company of
Kindness.

SARCASM is A dANgeROUS WEAPON...

FINd ANOtheR wAy to deliver youR MESSAGe.

sometimes A hANdwRitteN letteR cAN do this FoR you withont FAce-mAkiNg ANd toNe oF Uoice complicAtioNs.

TREAT
NASTY
Gossip
exactly like what
you gather and
place in large
plastic bags for
weekly pickup. Do
Not share, dolly!

trash

xox

GARBAGE

MASTER the
PATIENT
ART
oF
Listening
And being Fully
present...

THEN darlin, you

will be Heard.

In all relationships,
the person who remains
silent
is least likely (you can
bet your piggy bank on
this) to get what they
silently
wish for... SPEAK

UP,
dolly.
L.

WAY
up.

P.S. Mind reading is an overrated
folly.

Do not strike
Living Things...
Instead
dARLiN...
Punch the wind,
scold the prickly pines...
skip slippery stones
from one LAke to
Another.
Learn to Hold the
tempest
in your TEAPOT.

Forgiveness
will
Free your Heart
darlin,
And let it Fly
Above All of those
who Relish in the
hateful sport of
trying to break
Hearts...
Be AN exquisite
Butterfly.

uH oh...

CARRYING A KING-KONG SIZE
Grudge
CAN breAk your bAck
well before osteoponosis
sAys hello.

IMAgine dropping it
OFF At the GRAND
CANYON for A long
dive into NOWHERE.
Let it go, sweet dARlin,
And join LiFe's best
PicNic.

PEACE

All human beings
have good in them...
All human beings.
Animals, of course, are
PERFect.

Keep your Temples,
physical And spiritual,
Nice
And tidy...
fresh And neat.
A routine of clean
sweeping
is A good idea.

whooosh!

whoosh

whooosh

BEWARE

The Escape of
Drugs
★
can be a very
unpleasant, darker-
than-dark Sinkhole...
with no Return ticket.
Not even for the
sweet naive likes of
Dorothy
And
Toto!!

ORiginally

What you see, darlin,

is

usually

only PART of what you
get. Those <u>other PARTs</u>...
Are what might take most
of your Attention down
life's

Ziggin
Z A g g i n

Road.

Hold on

OH My!!!

detour →
2347 miles

DEFERRED GRATIFICATION is not just FOR those serving time in PRISON.

TRY A little bit of this in your credit card life, dolly!!

2000 +

discipline...
highly, highly
underrated;
the blue chip
stock of
tomorrow.

Do not create
the debt headache.

Never laugh at Frugality...
It will serve you well if and
when the money tree in
your meadow of dreams
skips a season, due to
unexpected
FROST.

A Hot Fudge
Sundae
is A Mighty Nice
thing to have on
A Not-so hot-fudgy
day.

USE
your Abundant
And blessed IMAGINATION
daily. This, darlin,
will SAVE you. It's
Not An expensive
store-bought Treatment.
It is yours Alone, And
only IF it is not
used will it cost you
dearly.

SANITY

FEAR
is a hard test
to FACE. Trust
your instincts, and
if you feel like
a doe caught in
headlights ...
Remember these words
in your mother's
loudest, bossiest voice.

RUN
baby, RUN !! !

Life,
sweetheart

is a solitary and

personal expedition

in search of the balance

between Bald Eagle
Freedom

And our desire to be

connected to each other

like bubblegum on a

Sunny-day Sneaker!

FACE

your lessons and challenges HEAD-ON. Own what is yours— battle sorrows, spend joy generously. Fix what is Fixable... PRONto... before the junkyard knows you by Name.

Borrowed
Monies Are
often owned over
long spells of time.
Interest can be
pricier than first
thought when desire
is your guide.

the
BANK
Loves
collecting
interest,
in
their
interest.

When you think
you do not have
what you NEED or
WANT...
Simply,
with grace...
your unique grace...
MAke do,
darlin,
MAKE do !!!

be creative

Every single year, once or twice, plan and take a real vacation! ¢ ¢ ¢ Even if it's in your own backyard. A vacation means vacating your heart and soul of work and routine worry... so that you can return REFReshed.

So far, darlin, the only thing on earth that keeps on ticking... Non-stop is a Timex®.

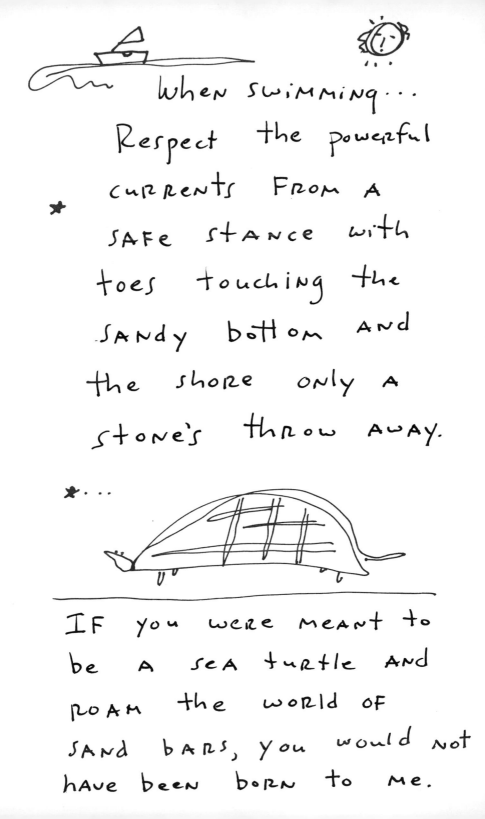

When swimming...
Respect the powerful
currents from a
safe stance with
toes touching the
sandy bottom and
the shore only a
stone's throw away.

If you were meant to
be a sea turtle and
roam the world of
sand bars, you would not
have been born to me.

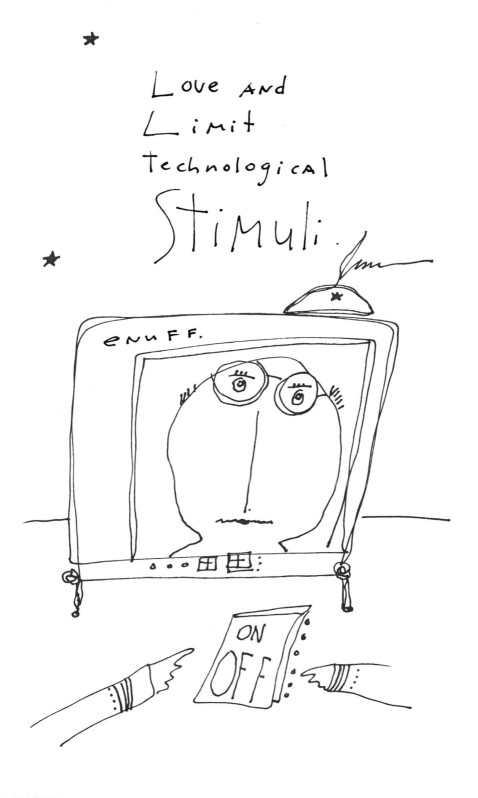

All people play parts
in their own personal
SOAP OPERAS !
Those on TV are mild
versions of Reality-
Reruns. Pick your
Roles with care.

HERO, LEADER, JERK,
WiMP, PARty girl,
FRuitCAke, Angel,
Sweet Heart.

OSCAR CARE

PRActice
youR giFt oF
HuMOR...

LAugh outloud, joke,
gently tease, TuRN
eAch Minus into A
RARe plus. You cAN
do this dolly. It's
A HAppy IRick, you
AlReAdy KNow!!!

HONOR YOUR WORD AND WEAR A WATCH.

I do promise to keep my promises.

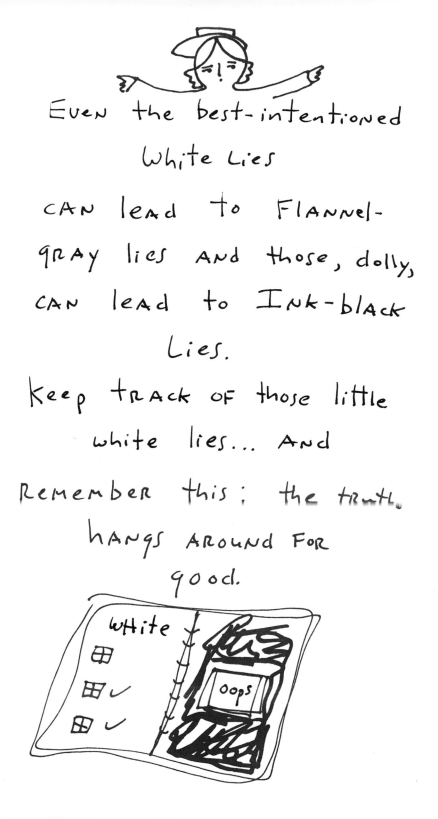

Even the best-intentioned
White Lies

can lead to Flannel-
gray lies and those, dolly,
can lead to Ink-black
Lies.

Keep track of those little
white lies... And

Remember this: the truth
hangs around for
good.

D A R L i N !!

CHEATiNG
is
veRy, VERy bAd foR
youR Good self. ANy
gAiNs will be lost
iN A bliNk to the
tiReless tRuth
of... CHEATeR's Blues...

OLIVIA'S SUPERIOR PAIN NUMBER

It's really best not to rely on over-the-counter drugs for fixing problems that hang around. See a Doctor.

Trust A PRO!

Feel Free of course to call Me First!

SEARCH And you shall Find!

SORROW is part of Life's Magnificent Banquet... A little bit will not hurt you. A lot may change you and challenge you... But never, ever FEAR!! This glorious banquet offers unlimited Joy and sustenance for the taking, darlin... For your taking.

xox

No matter how
many times your
Heart has known
Betrayal...
Trust Again.
Begin Again.

WHEN you hEAR
A distANt siReN...
sAy A petite pRAyeR.

pRAyeR, dARliN,
is A ReAl
CONVeRSAtioN
with youR
DiviNe MAKeR
who is kiNd
ANd loving.
ANd
you ARe A
FAUORite!

cHAt it up... we ARe
All
coNNected.

FIND YOUR CHURCH...

KNOW YOUR GOD...

Believe in Heaven.

PONDER the PROMISE OF
LiFe AND PARTICIPATE well.

MELT UNFAIR gender
bARRieRS AS you live
A LiFe OF PuRpose.
CombAt RACiSM... AND
All other bReAches
oF the HuMAN HeARt.
Become A moderN-dAy
HeRoiNe
iN SNeAkeRS.
youR mother AND
EleANoR Roosevelt
would be PRouD!!
veRy
pRoud.

*

Try not to stare
like a deer in
Headlights at
people who look and
Act differently.
Respect their space
And uniqueness.

ooops

Sweet darlin...
Treat all beings with
Royal kindness...
be they a cafeteria
server or janitor...
fire fighter or cab
driver. And if you
do indeed meet crowned
blue-bloods... treat
them as everyday people
blessed with their own
kind of hard job... just
like the rest of us.

Pick up AFTER youR
sweet selF (there ARe
No peRsoNAl 24-HouR
FaiRies iN ReAl liFe).
EveN iF you ARe
At the Ritz... be
Respectful of those
iN seRvice... they
ARe people; someones
motheR, sisteR, fRiend.

Tip those
who serve you well.
Pretend that no
matter the season...
it's a jolly Christmas
EVE.

Dolly... when you are a guest in Another's Abode... always take a gift of thanks... perhaps a nice African violet plant or box of locally-made chocolates. After the visit, follow-up pronto with a hand-penned note!!

xox

FINE HOMEMADE sweets

*   Do not judge
People by a messy
car! Some things
just have to give,
darlin!!

WASH
Me!

CHoose ReAl
Beauty ... FoRged
by A HAnd thAt
is coNNected to the
HeARt ANd MARRied
to the soul.

As you walk down
a road, sidewalk,
or sandy beach path,
bend down and pick
up any trash that
may present its
unwelcome self This
only takes a moment
and you will feel
terrific!

preserve
beauty,
darlin.

TRy
HARd

Not to eat all of
your meals in the
CAR...
Traffic, horn-tooting,
And Fast-braking
moves Are hardly
friends of good
digestion.

.....Some Rituals Are
worth keeping!

DRINK

PLENTY OF PURE WATER...

it will keep you WELL, darlin. Very WELL indeed.

yum

* Visit the
DENTist ev**e**ry
S**in**gle year !!

* Those braces and
lost Retainers were
not a feeble Attempt
by your mother to
enjoy free Reading
of PEOPLE magazines.

* PEOPLE
——————
volume #
2 zillion

*

P.S. did I mention
the broken Hoover® that
found your retainer?

Talking crossly
(like a raving loon)
to drivers who annoy
you and cannot hear
you is a tedious
exercise... Plus, if
you are not alone
in your car, a
brutish faux pas.

HUSH

P.S. pretend the seasoned
drivers are your geezer
parents... Have mercy !!!

When you must change LANes... Always Remember to take the NANosecond to LOOK in your blind spot (we all have them). And Remember that your seat belt is not a FAshion Accessory.

Life can be the greatest circus on earth. As with amusement parks, it's good to balance out the slower rides with the wilder ones and the FREAK SHOWS with a quiet moment, sitting on a bench, watching the world go by ... cotton candy and all. Remember, dolly, even the merriest of merry-go-rounds can wind down to a sad stop.... if not given respite.

*...

In order for you to live a life with both feet touching the ground, you need to converse fluently (on a regular basis) with NATURE!!!

Please take note of these hotlines... and chit-chat!!

wind

stars

Pines

sky

butterflies

Mountains

Lakes

Streams

In the Hot, Hot Summer
of Sandcastles... Stay
Long darlin At the
beAch. Until the sun
drops like A gigantic
golden egg into the seA.
Rest And build A city
of dreAms with whAteveR
is within your hAnd's
ReAch. Sometimes that
is moRe thAn youR
deAR heArt will eveR
Need... just whAt is
within youR hAnd's ReAch.

Trust
your
Intuitive
Pilot

It has a built-in
radar system that
makes NASA look like
a corny walkie-talkie
from the '50s.

DARK,

dark indigo days
will eventually, darlin,
give way to blue
skies... where the
only clouds are
soft magic carpets,
ready to Fly your
dreams come
TRUE.

It's OK to wear the purple cloak of "I'm Feeling sooo sorry for MYSELF!" as long as, after a whirl or two, you put it back in the closet and wear the nice RED CABLEknit sweater with green Bakelite bow buttons... you know, darlin, the "I CAN DO THIS AND BEGIN AGAIN" one.

If you find yourself in A miserable money crunch, unable to pay All of the bills on time... Give each party A little something in good Faith Along with A Note of explanation And Apology that Assures them of your intent to pay. Never ignore Reality, dARLiN, it will only vanish when you FAce it.

Let your mistakes
fine-tune the compass
deep inside your
HEART...
so that you will
have splendid travels
worthy of
a kind and wise
SOULFUL
SELF!

Guilt and shame
do not belong in
your wardrobe
of feelings...
wear pride, self-
respect, and love...
Pitch
should've
could've
would've
and
what if only.

xox

Do Something for
Someone or more
than one Someone...
Without
expecting or wanting
ANything
in Return. And
Bingo,
dolly, your Life will
be Richer than Rich!

When you are Perched with Lofty Power...

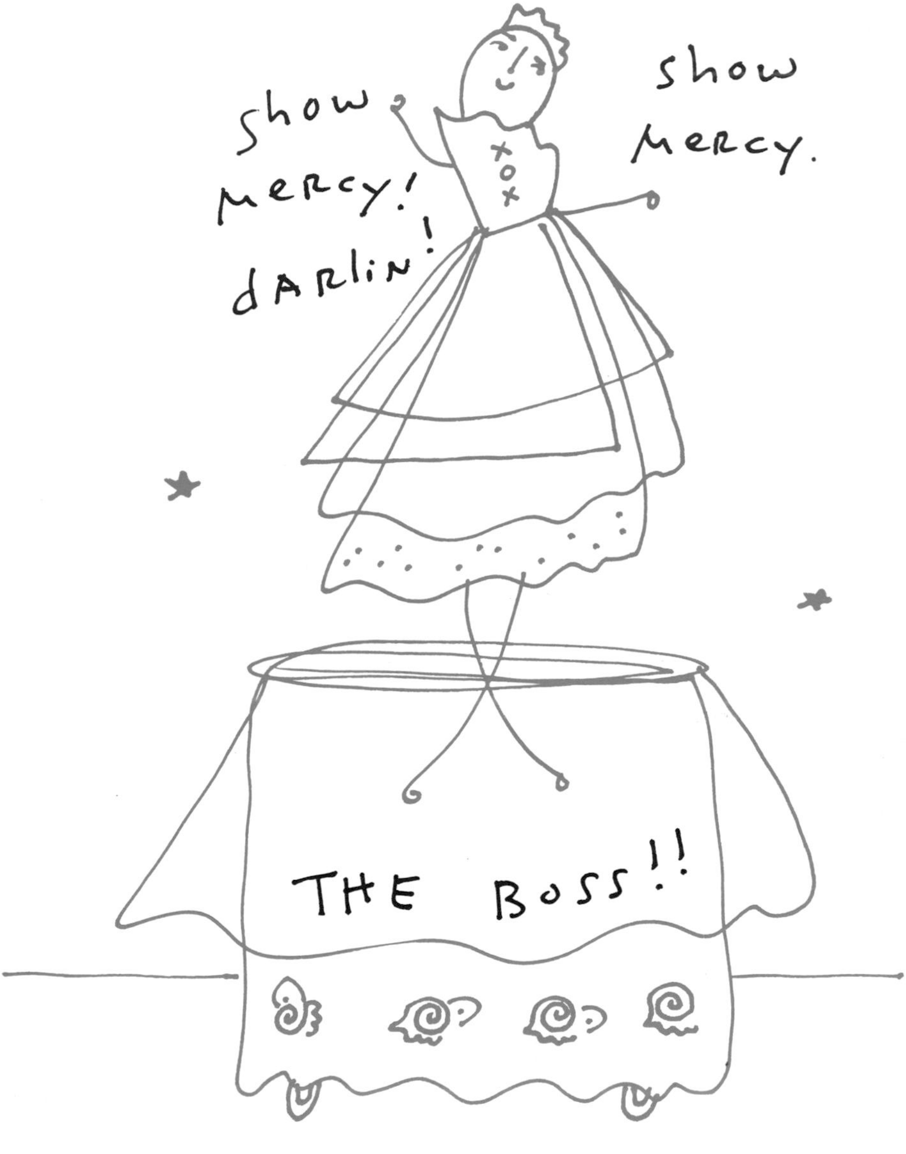

You are never too
old
for a
Nice leisurely

Moonbeam
Bath in the evening
time.

Necessary items.

A blanket

A starry night

A wide-awake self,
Horizontally
floating a weebit
above this
sweet earth.

A cup of cinnamon
tea with a sprig
of hope... and
dream

Some days are
meant
to be spent
doing absolutely

Nothing,

Nothing at

All.

And that, darlin, can be
the best present you
treat yourself to.

Home all day,
just me, myself,
and I.

*

Keep a list that will
not fade from sight of
all those dear folks
that have loved you
into bloom. Remember
to remind them of
their perpetual gifts.
(Of course darlin,
they know because
<u>you</u> are the most
vivid reminder.) <u>Still</u>
never remain quiet.
A card, a phone call...
an unexpected visit.
These small thank yous
MUST BE.

CALL HOME, Sweet dARliN... AS often AS YouR Bizee Heart desires! And then double it for your mother And triple it for your FATher!

RING-A-LING-A-LING!!

Siblings Are A Huge Bonus. dolly! Sow together A garden of Loving Curiosity And Reap A Harvest of wonder to carry through Adulthood.

LONESOME, you will NEVER BE!

Discover the
Mystery
of
Love!!

It may take some major
archaeological
digs...

But, darlin... when you
Find it, the
TREASURE
of a lifetime will be
yours.

I promise!

TRue BLue...
FoReveR
SApphire BLue!!
Love does hAppen, dolly!
Look
FoR it
Above All other lustre...
kindness
HuMoR
loyAlty
Respect
And A sterling devotion
to "us" And "we."

sweet doll-bAby of Mine,

Before you hAve

children...

buy A Nice, FLuFFy

Scottie

And see how it goes.

RuFF-RuFF
BAY-bee!!

2%

Shampoo

vet

bone

treats

I can still hear
my dear Grandmother
Maize say, "Never, darlin,
ever go to bed mad
at your mate!"

Try and do better at
this than your mother
did.

NO MATTER HOW
FAR AWAY I MAY
seem to you, it
simply is not so...
I AM RIGHT HERE
beside you... Loving
your sweet heart
every single minute.
Because you ARE MY GIRL!

And you know your
Mother ALWAYS MEANS
WHAt she SAYS, dARliN.
Don't You!?

I have a secret to tell you. I think you are old enough to handle tHis now. A mother annoys her children with a constant litany of advice, not because she is daffy or in a pre-Alzheimer fog. She repeats herself because she loves you and realizes how very busy you have been growing up and that you might have been distracted.

Wisdom is not hereditary, sweet daughter of Mine.

* Common sense cannot be ordered via catalogue or E-mail. It's all up to you now... Go and find what really, really matters on this earth. You are so ready! I love you.

xox

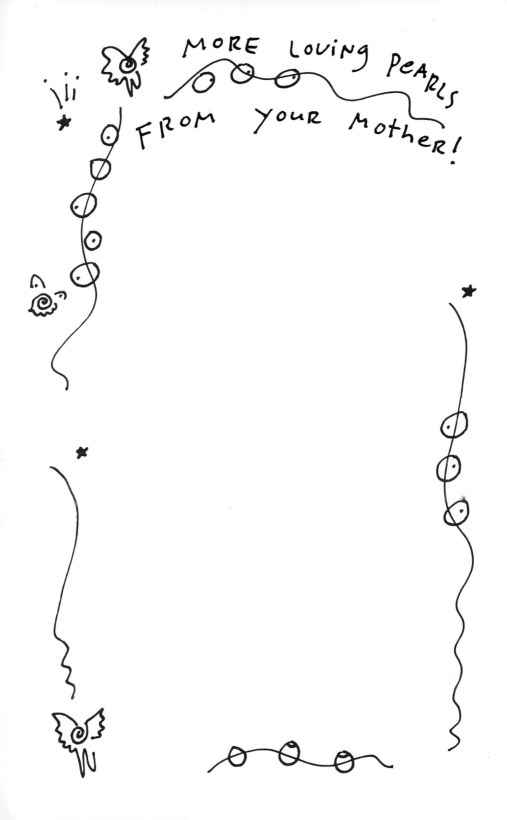

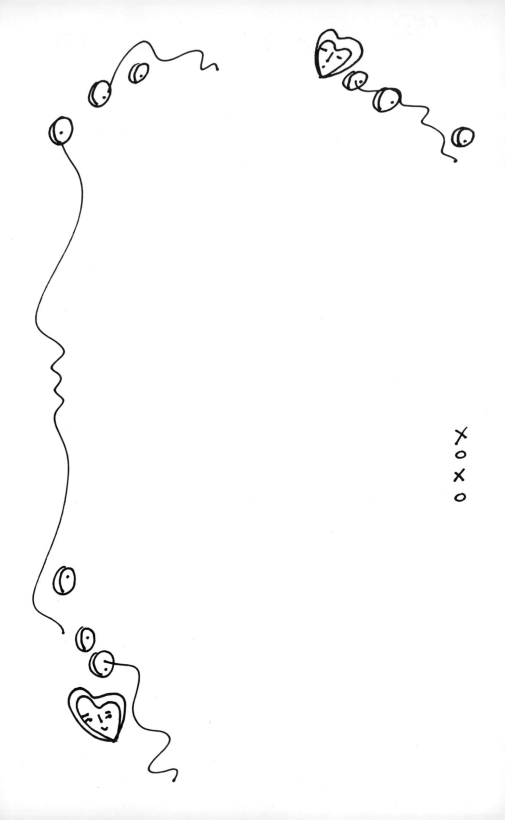

XOXO

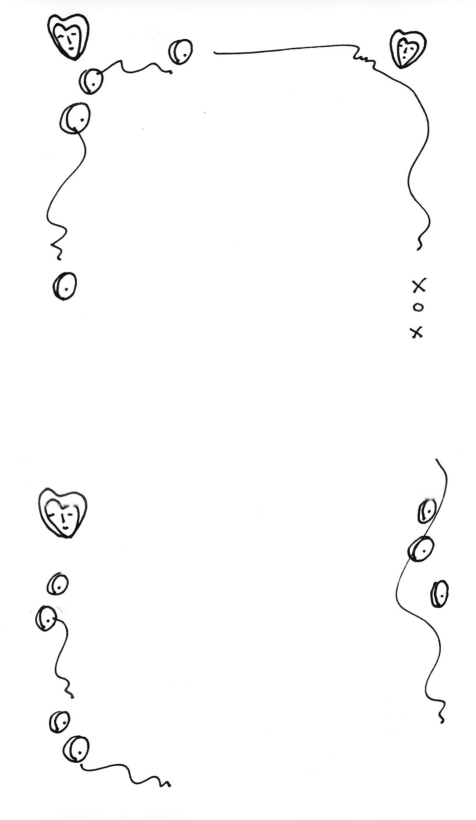

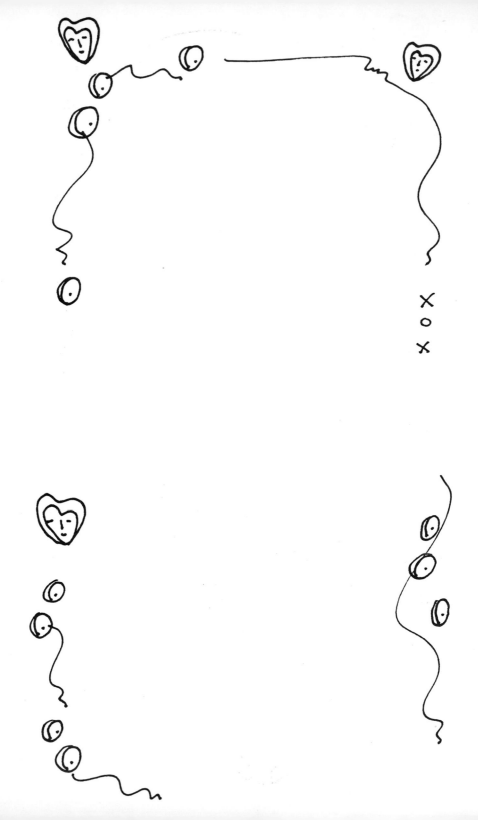

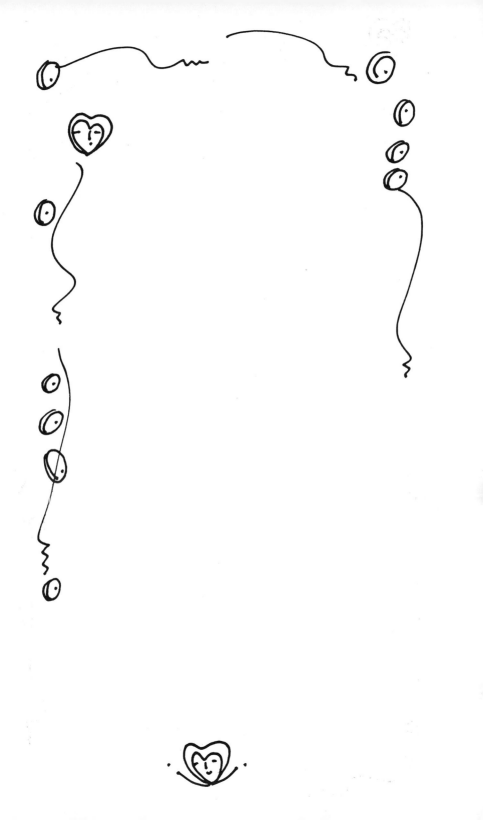

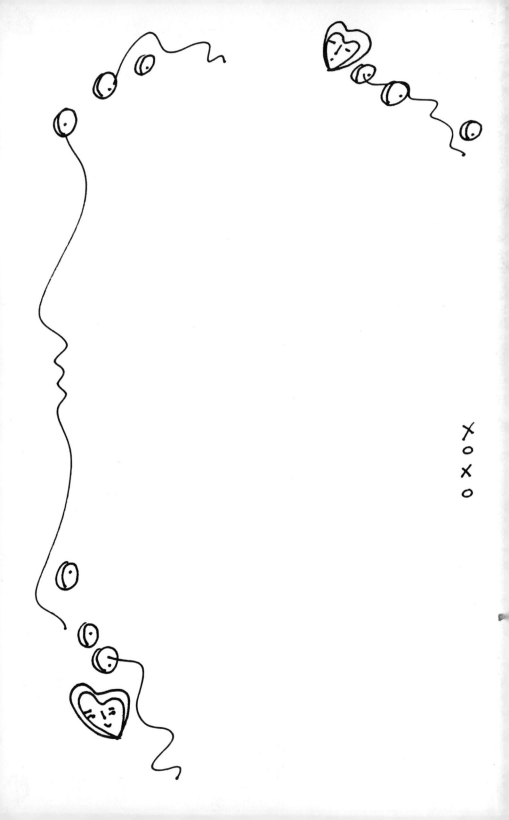

xoxo

About the Author And Artist...

Nancy Swan Drew is in her heart of a zillion hearts a mother 🫀 enormously blessed with daughters— those spirits that give purpose and light to a mother's soul.

*

Other Books by
Nancy Swan Drew

The Artful Spirit
First-Aid Kit for Mothers
Be Your own Angel

*

She can be reached at:
www.NANCYSWANDREW.com